Event
197_

The Top News Stories of the Year

By Hugh Morrison

Montpelier Publishing
London

ISBN-13: 978-1984146816
ISBN-10: 1984146815
Published by Montpelier Publishing, London.
Printed and distributed by Amazon Createspace.
This edition © 2018. All rights reserved.

Events of
1978

Sid Vicious of 'The Sex Pistols'

Crown without a king

Hungary's crown jewels returned after 33 years

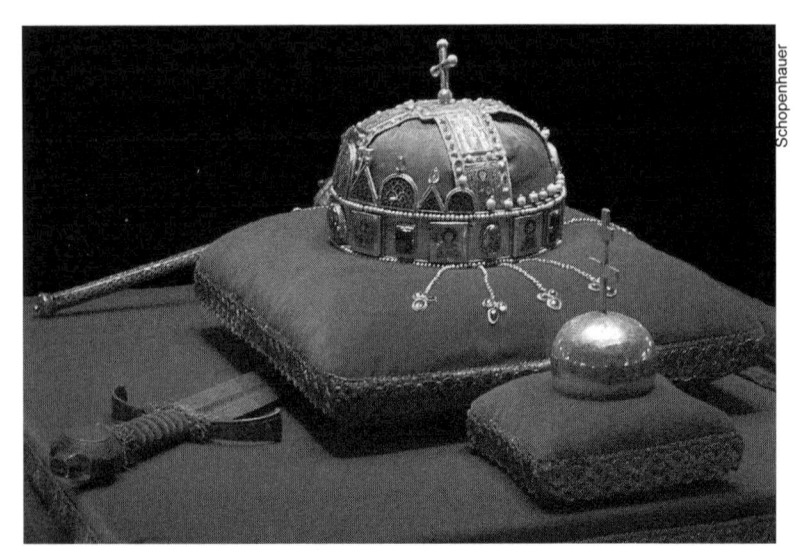

On the feast of Epiphany, 6 January 1978 the Hungarian crown jewels, including the crown of St Stephen dating from the eleventh century, were finally returned to their homeland.

Although the last king to wear the crown went into exile following the First World War, Hungary remained a Regency, (a 'kingdom without a king') until the Communists took over after the Second World War. Thus the crown jewels had, and still have, enormous symbolic significance for many Hungarians.

In 1945 as the Russians approached Budapest, the jewels were hidden by the Hungarian Crown Guard, and later recovered by the US Army at Mattsee in Austria. They were then taken to Fort Knox in the USA for safekeeping where they were also subject to extensive authentication tests.

As US-Hungarian relations improved in the 1970s, President Jimmy Carter ordered that the jewels be returned, and a US delegation saw them installed in the Hungarian parliament building in Budapest, where they remain.

Fire when ready

Fire Brigade strike ends after three months

Firemen across the UK finally went back to work on 12 January 1978 after a three month long strike. Unions had demanded a 30% pay increase but the government would not move beyond 10% and the unions eventually reluctantly accepted this.

Troops had provided cover for the duration of the strik, often insufficiently trained and equipped with outdated technology such as 1950s Green Goddess fire engines, kept in reserve after the disbanding of the volunteer Auxiliary Fire Service in 1968. Soldiers averted a major catastrophe on Merseyside when they stopped a haulage depot blaze at Kirkdale spreading to a 500-gallon petrol storage tank.

Some firefighters did break the strike, particularly during a fire at St Andrew's hospital in London.

Below: Royal Marines with a 1950s Green Goddess Auxiliary Fire Service engine.

Bug gets squashed

Last Volkswagen Beetle (Bug) built in Germany

The Volkwagen Beetle (Bug) above and right, its successor the Golf (Rabbit).

16 January 1978 marked the end of the road for the iconic Volkswagen Beetle, known as the Bug in the USA, as production ended in Germany.

The distinctive small car based on designs by Ferdinand Porsche had been launched in the 1930s but the factory was nearly ruined in the Second World War. The occupying British Army of the Rhine, however, saw the potential of the little car for officer transport and restarted production, setting it on the road to worldwide fame and over 21 million sales.

By the 1970s the pre-war technology of the vehicle was badly dated, and in 1974 Volkswagen launched its successor, the Golf hatchback, known in the USA as the Rabbit.

Like its British counterpart the Mini, however, the Beetle refused to die – production continued in Latin America and the last Beetle was built in Mexico in 2003.

The weather outside is frightful
The Great Blizzard of 1978

Also known as the White Hurricane, the Great Blizzard of 1978 was one of the worst weather events on record to hit the northeastern USA.

Up to 40 inches of snow fell on Wisconsin, and winds of over 100 mph were recorded. Wind-chilled temperatures dropped to -60F (-51C) in Ohio, where up to 70 people died as a result of the storm. Canada was also affected, with 16 inches of snow falling on London, Ontario.

Much of the northeastern USA was paralysed with a state of emergency declared in Michigan, where the National Guard (territorials) were mobilised, and police called for volunteers with 4x4s to help evacuate the injured to hospitals.

The storm itself lasted from 25 to 27 January but the snowfall in some places was so heavy that people were trapped in their houses for up to a week afterwards.

Traffic snowed under on Route 128 near Needham, Massachussetts. In Indiana, police closed the entire state's road network due to heavy snowfall.

'Yorkshire Ripper' strikes again

Three victims in 1978

Peter Sutcliffe, the serial killer dubbed the Yorkshire Ripper, claimed three victims in 1978 as part of his eleven year reign of terror in which he murdered thirteen women.

Sutcliffe brutally murdered 21 year old prostitute Yvonne Pearson on 21 January 1978 in Bradford in the north of England, after which he unsuccessfully hid her body in a lane.

Ten days later he murdered 18 year old Helen Rytka, also a prostitute, in Huddersfield, bludgeoning her to death with a hammer and again unsuccessfully concealing the corpse under a railway arch. Sutcliffe's final victim of 1978 was Vera Millward, who was killed in Manchester. The Ripper did not strike again until April 1979.

Extensive police investigations to find the killer had been going on for years, but Sutcliffe was only finally found by chance in January 1981, when a police constable spotted the false number plates on his car.

Following his arrest, police found incriminating weapons and Sutcliffe confessed to his crimes. Following a sensational trial, was committed for life to Broadmoor Hospital for the criminally insane, but was declared no longer mentally ill in 2016 and transferred to Frankland Prison in Durham.

Fans catch fever

Bee Gees hit *Night Fever* is top of the charts

Disco track *Night Fever* was a smash hit for British band the Bee Gees. It first appeared on the soundtrack of the John Travolta film *Saturday Night Fever* the previous year, but was not released as a single until 1978.

Written by the Bee Gees themselves – brothers Barry, Robin and Maurice Gibb – the song was inspired by Percy Faith's famous orchestral sixties hit, *Theme From A Summer Place.*

The song topped the UK singles chart for two weeks, and in the US it remained the number one Billboard Hot 100 single for over two months. Billboard magazine ranked it as the second best song of 1978, after the non-Bee Gee brother Andy Gibb's *Shadow Dancing*, and it was the third of six consecutive US number one hits for the band, which equals the record set by the Beatles for the most consecutive number one hits.

Unusually for the time, a video of the song was also made, featuring the band in a studio interspersed with clips of Florida townscapes.

Right: the Bee Gees in 1978. From top: Barry, Robin and Maurice Gibb. Their song *Night Fever* was voted second best hit of 1978.

The man who beat Ali

Leon Spinks defeats boxing legend

Above: Leon Spinks.
Right: Muhammed Ali interviewed in 1978.

Boxing titan Muhammed Ali was defeated by up and coming fighter Leon Spinks in the Undisputed Heavyweight Championships held in Las Vegas on 15 February 1978.

Spinks made history by winning the world heavyweight title after only eight professional fights, the shortest time in history.

The ageing Ali, who was ten years Spinks' senior, was out-boxed by the younger man who also went down in history as the only man to take a title from Ali in the ring, with all his other defeats being in non-title fights.

Ali, however, was back with a vengeance at a rematch on 15 September in Louisiana, where things went badly for Spinks.

Ali was in better shape than in the previous bout and was able to win his title back, becoming the first three-time lineal heavyweight champion.

Ali announced his retirement from boxing after the fight, although he did make brief comebacks in later years. Spinks went on to have a long career in boxing and also made a brief foray into wrestling in the 1990s.

Last days of the Raj
Paul Scott, author of *The Jewel in the Crown*, dies

The last great chronicler of the British Raj colonial era in India died on 1 March 1978. Paul Scott, (born 1920) was the author of *The Raj Quartet,* a series of novels of British India which were to become famous in the 1980s when they were adapted for television as *The Jewel in the Crown.*

Unlike many of the characters that he created, Scott did not come from an old Anglo-Indian family but was born into a relatively humble background in a north London suburb.

After conscription into the army as a private in 1940, he showed sufficient promise to be commissioned as an officer in the Indian Army. It was at this time that his long love affair with the subcontinent began.

On his return to Britain after the end of the war, Scott began writing novels chronicling the war and the sunset of British rule in India, and the racial and class conflicts involved in the wind-down of the Raj. He achieved his first success in 1952 with Indian Army war novel *Johnny Sahib*, and completed his magnum opus, *The Jewel in the Crown*, not in India but in his house in suburban north London.

His novel *Staying On*, the epilogue to the Raj Quartet, won the Booker Prize in 1977. Made into a film with Trevor Howard and Celia Johnson in 1980, it is a touching portrait of a British couple living out their twilight years in post-colonial India.

Nothing sacred

Grave robbers steal Charlie Chaplin's body

One of the most famous cases of body-snatching occurred on 2 March 1978, when the body of comedian Charlie Chaplin (1889-1977) was stolen from its grave in the village of Corsier-sur-Vevey, near Lausanne, Switzerland.

Chaplin's widow Oona received a ransom demand $600,000 for the return of his corpse. Police were informed and a large investigation began, with 200 phone boxes in the region put under observation. Mrs Chaplin refused to pay the demand, after which the criminals threatened to harm her children.

After five weeks police tracked down the grave robbers: Roman Wardas, a Pole, and Gantscho Ganev, a Bulgarian, both asylum seekers working as car mechanics.

They led police to Chaplin's body which they had removed to a hidden grave about a mile from its original resting place. Wardas was sentenced to four and half years' hard labour, and Ganev received an 18-month suspended sentence due to his limited involvement.

Chaplin was reburied in a concrete covered tomb to prevent any further sacrilege.

Chaplin was reburied in a concrete covered tomb (left) in Corsier-sur-Vevey, Switzerland.

The Hitchhiker's Guide to the Galaxy

Cult comedy first broadcast on BBC

Above: Author Douglas Adams (1952-2001)

On 8 March 1978 the first episode was broadcast of what was to become a long running cult science fiction comedy series: *The Hitchhiker's Guide to the Galaxy* by Douglas Adams.

The series, which started out on BBC Radio, follows the adventures of hapless Englishman Arthur Dent and his alien friend Ford Prefect, a writer for the pan-galactic travel guide *The Hitchhiker's Guide to the Galaxy.*

Earth is destroyed in the first episode, and the pair travel the galaxy encountering numerous comic characters such as Slartibartfast and Zaphod Beeblebrox.

In addition to sending up the budget travel guides of the 1970s, the show makes fun of sci-fi cliches and also takes a Pythonesque view of man's place in the universe. Probably the most famous joke in that vein is when Dent finds out the meaning of life – which turns out to be the number 42!

The series was developed into three highly successful books, a TV series, cinema film and live tour and remains highly popular to this day.

Aldo Moro murdered
Red Brigade kidnaps and kills Italian PM

Italian Prime Minister Aldo Moro (born 1916) was kidnapped on 16 March 1978 in Rome by members of the far left Red Brigade (*Brigate Rosse*) who killed his five bodyguards while doing so. Over the following days security forces made hundreds of raids nationwide to try to find him, without success.

The Red Brigade demanded the release from prison of several of its members in return for Moro. The government refused to negotiate, and event the Pope released a statement urging the kidnappers to give up. Eventually Moro, who had been held in an apartment in Rome, was shot ten times and his body was left in a car near the River Tiber in Rome.

After a series of arrests a Red Brigade member, Mario Moretti, confessed to the killing and was sentenced to life imprisonment. The following year, Marxist philosopher Antonio Negri, thought to be the mastermind of the Red Brigade, was arrested and the gang's reign of terror came to an end.

Left: Aldo Moro while being held for ransom. Below: Moro's assassin, Mario Moretti.

Oil soap cleans up

Dallas becomes immediate hit

Above: Southfork Ranch.
Right: *Dallas* star JR Ewing (Larry Hagman)

On 2 April 1978 US audiences were introduced to the wealthy world of Texan oil barons the Ewing family, headed by big-hat wearing bully JR Ewing, played by Larry Hagman. The series focused on the rivalry between the Ewings and Barnes families, with much of the action taking place on the Southfork Ranch.

The show was an instant hit and 'JR' soon became the star; when he was shot in 1980 the show became the second highest ever rated broadcast.

In on episode, principal character Bobby Ewing was killed off – but audiences were so unhappy about this that the character was brought back in the following series. The writers got round this problem of resurrection by showing that the entire previous series had been dreamed by Ewing's wife!

Unusually for an American soap opera, the show was popular in many other countries, including in such unlikely places as Romania where it was originally broadcast as a warning against capitalism!

The show spawned a spin off series, *Knots Landing*, plus two TV movies and a revival series in 2012-2014.

Four Oscars for *Annie Hall*

Woody Allen film is critical success

Woody Allen's romantic comedy *Annie Hall* was one of the smash cinema hits of 1977. Accordingly on 3 April 1978 it was recognised at the Academy Awards with four Oscars. Set in New York City, the film tells the story of the relationship between comedian Alvie Singer (Woody Allen) and Annie Hall (Diane Keaton).

The couple move in together and all goes well at first but eventually the relationship breaks down and the film looks back on what went wrong, both in Alvie's life with Annie and with his former lovers.

The film will be familiar to fans of Woody Allen with its themes of neurosis, Jewish identity, psychotherapy, and the lives of New York's artistic/intellectual set. Departing from cinematic convention, Allen breaks the 'fourth wall' and addresses the audience directly, and a similar scene occurs when the couple are queuing to see a film and overhear an argument between two men about the work of writer Marshall McLuhan. McLuhan himself then steps forward from his place in the queue to set the matter straight.

In addition to winning four Oscars it was nominated for a further five, although it was beaten in the Best Picture category by *Rocky*. In the British Academy of Film and Television Arts (BAFTA) Awards it won Best Film.

The Writers' Guild of America went further, and declared it the 'funniest ever film' in its list of 101 top comedies.

A man, a plan, a canal: Panama

US agrees to handover by 1999

On 7 September 1977 the USA and Panama signed the Torrijos-Carter Treaties, guaranteeing that the US control of the canal would be handed over to Panama by 1999. The treaties were named after the two signatories, US President Jimmy Carter and General Omar Torrijos of Panama.

The Panama Canal is of vital civil and military importance, as it forms a short cut between the Atlantic and Pacific oceans saving thousands of miles of travel around south America. Originally started by the French, the canal was taken over by the US who completed it in 1914. After the Suez Canal was taken over by Egyptians in 1956, efforts for a similar nationalisation by Panama began in earnest, resulting in riots in 1963 in which 20 people were killed, and diplomatic relations between the US and Panama were broken off.

Over the following years negotiations resumed and eventually a mutually satisfactory treaty was drawn up, but Carter was criticised in some quarters for giving up a valuable US asset to a head of state (Torrijos) who was not democratically elected.

President Carter (left) meets General Torrijos of Panama.

The Blues Brothers

Cult musical comedians first appear

Cult musical duo the Blues Brothers made their first appearance on 22 April 1978 as the musical guest stars on US TV's *Saturday Night Live*. Elwood and Jake Blues, played respectively by comedians Dan Aykroyd and John Belushi, performed the song *Hey Bartender*.

The band went on to release an album the same year which went double platinum, but they really hit the big time in 1980 when they starred in the blockbuster Hollywood movie *The Blues Brothers*, about the pair's madcap dash across the USA to save an orphanage. The band and the movie developed cult status, particularly after Belushi's untimely death in 1982. Since then it has been on numerous live tours and made many TV appearances. A second film followed in 2000: *Blues Brothers 2000: The Blues are Back*. The band reformed for a world tour in 1988 and again in 1998.

The band has spawned a host of imitators, lookalikes, tribute acts and artistic works, such as the above piece of grafitti art from Poland.

Kabul turns Saur

Saur Revolution in Afghanistan

On 27 April 1978 a military coup took place in Afghanistan, when the People's Democratic Party took power in what is known as the Saur Revolution after the Persian name of the month in which it occurred.

The country had only recently undergone a previous coup, when King Zahir Shah was ousted by Mohammed Daoud Khan in 1973. Factions and rivalries developed during Daoud's government, and the military decided to seize power on a Thursday evening as they knew many officials were off duty in preparation for Friday, the Islamic holy day. Insurgents attacked the presidential palace in the capital Kabul, killing Daoud and his family.

Troops appeared on the streets and fighting broke out between police and military; by evening a formal announcement was made on Radio Afghanistan that the government had been overthrown.

The new regime was not popular, and crushed dissent ruthlessly. The presence of such a danger on its doorstep prompted the Soviet Union to invade in 1979, leading to a long and bitter conflict.

The Presidential Palace in Kabul, where Daoud Khan (inset) was assassinated.

WACs: dismissed!

Women's Army Corps joins the men

Above: Colonel Oveta Culp Hobby, the first WAC commanding officer.
Right: WAC signal operators in WW2.

In 1978 the Women's Army Corps was disbanded and all female units were integrated with male units of the US Army. This brought to an end an institution that had been set up in the Second World War and which had fought proudly for its country – and also for its reputation.

Based on all-female units in the British army, the WAC was set up when the USA joined the Second World War in 1942. Initially an auxiliary force only, it gained full active service status in 1943. The intention was to free up men from non-combatant roles, so women were put into signals, mechanics, armoury and clerical roles. There was initial hostility in some quarters, with senior military officials questioning their competence, but the WACs gradually proved themselves invaluable to the war effort.

The incorporation into male units in 1978 was probably an inspiration for one of the comedy successes of the early 1980s, the film and TV series *Private Benjamin* starring Goldie Hawn. Women in the US army were not permitted to engage in frontline combat, however, until 1994.

Operation Reindeer

South African army engages in Angola

From 1966 to 1990 South Africa fought a war of territorial dispute on its borders with Namibia, Zambia and Angola, principally against the South West African People's Organisation (SWAPO), a Namibian nationalist movement.

As part of this conflict, Operation Reindeer began on 4 May 1978, a major military engagement in Angola. Attacks were made on two SWAPO bases at Chetequera and Dombondola, and then controversially, an airborne assault was carried out by paratroopers on SWAPOs regional headquarters at Cassinga, which UNICEF had claimed also housed a refugee camp.

International journalists invited by Angola photographed mass graves of what appeared to be civilians on the site, but the South Africans maintained these were irregular Namibian military combatants who had not been uniformed.

The operation ended on 10 May 1978.

South African troops in the Border War.

Ipswich win FA Cup

Outsiders triumph in football final

Ipswich Town's Roger Osborne scored the winning goal at Wembley Stadium.

One of football's occasional unexpected turns took place on 6 May 1978 at the FA Cup Final at Wembley Stadium when East Anglian team Ipswich Town beat Arsenal 1-0.

Ipswich were the underdogs, having been beaten 6-1 by Aston Villa the previous Saturday, and were expected to be easy prey for the London opposition. To considerable surprise, however, Ipswich dominated the game. The winning goal was scored by Roger Osborne, who was so overcome by emotion at his success that fainted and had to be substituted. Following the match the team received a rapturous welcome in their home town, and fans flocked to buy copies of the team's hit single, *Ipswich Get That Goal.*

Ipswich were always something of an outsider team; they only joined the League in 1938 and did not make the First Division until 1960, under the guidance of the legendary Alf Ramsey. 1978 was probably the team's high water mark after which they returned to relative obscurity, although they did win the UEFA Cup in 1981.

Voyage to Venus

NASA explores the Green Planet

In 1978 NASA undertook the Pioneer Venus Project; an exploratory mission to the second planet.

The craft, *Pioneer Venus 1*, was the 8' diameter unmanned payload of a rocket launched on 20 May 1978. It entered Venusian orbit on 4 December 1978 and was able to send back data on Venus' topography and ground level atmosphere.

The craft then deployed four small probes into the Venusian atmosphere, one of which survived landing and transmitted data for an hour. It was not the first probe to do so; the Russians had got there first in 1970 with *Venera 7*, which had disappointed many sci-fi fans by showing that the planet was not able to support life.

The main craft remained in orbit and transmitted data for several years, including in 1986 when it was able to convey information on Halley's Comet. In October 1992 the craft's fuel supply ran out and it burnt up in the atmosphere of Venus.

An artists' impression of *Pioneer Venus 1* in orbit.

Place your bets

First legal casino in USA outside Nevada opens

Steve Lawrence and Eydie Gorme topped the bill at the Resorts Casino Hotel.

The Resorts Casino Hotel, the first legal casino outside of the state of Nevada, USA, opened in Atlantic City, New Jersey, on 26 May 1978.

Off-course betting and other forms of gambling were largely restricted in the USA to the state of Nevada, particularly Las Vegas. There were calls to allow gambling in other places, particularly due to the isolation of Nevada, with Atlantic City a favourite choice due to its proximity to New York. The casino and hotel was a conversion of two early twentieth century buildings, on the site of a much older hotel dating to the 1860s, with an entrance on the famous 'boardwalk'.

The hotel was wildly popular: long queues formed outside, partly due to the limited gambling hours. The hotel also featured a 1700 seat theatre, which opened with husband and wife singing duo Steve Lawrence and Eydie Gorme.

The lonely sea

NZ woman is first to sail solo round the world

Naomi James (*née* Power) became the first woman to sail single-handed around the world via Cape Horn, returning to Dartmouth, England, on 8 June 1978 after a journey of 272 days.

This was two days' faster than the record set by the first man to undertake the voyage, Sir Francis Chichester, in 1967.

Rather surprisingly, James did not have long experience of sailing; she grew up in the New Zealand countryside and did not begin to sail until 1975 after becoming engaged to a yachtsman, Rob James.

The *Daily Express* newspaper agreed to sponsor her attempt to sail round the world in the 53' yacht *Express Crusader*, and she successfully endured the rigours of the Clipper Route (the standard round the world route which crosses some of the world's most challenging seas) coping with the near loss of a mast, a capsizing, and a broken radio for several weeks.

Naomi James was made a Dame Commander of the Order of the British Empire in 1979 in recognition of her achievement.

James also took part in the Single Handed Trans-Atlantic Race in 1980, breaking the women's speed record with a time of 25 days. A further victory was won in 1982 after she and her husband Rob James won the Round Britain Race.

Tragically, Rob James drowned in a yachting accident in 1983, ten days before their daughter was born.

Grease is the word

Nostalgic musical is smash hit

Cinema-goers stepped back into the 1950s when the hit musical *Grease* opened on 16 June 1978; a nostalgic treat based on many of the mainstays of the 1950s high school movie genre, with 'hot rod' races, cheerleaders, ice-cream parlours and the 'prom'.

Based on a more bawdy 1971 off-Broadway stage musical, the film stars John Travolta (Danny) and Olivia Newton-John (Sandy) as high school kids who fall in love while on vacation in the summer of 1958 but then lose touch.

Danny and Sandy both enroll at Rydell High School the following autumn without knowing the other is there, and each give their respective groups of friends rather differing accounts of their holiday romance!

Sandy is horrified at the attack on her reputation but of course, true love always finds a way and in the end the pair successfully make compromises over their differing backgrounds and disappear into the sunset together.

The show is packed with hit songs including *You're the One That I Want, Greased Lightnin'* and *Hopelessly Devoted to You*.

A sequel, *Grease II* followed, and a soundtrack album, which was the second best selling album of 1978. The stage show has also been revived several times to packed houses.

Don't cry for me, Argentina

Andrew Lloyd Webber's *Evita* opens

Evita, by Andrew Lloyd Webber and Tim Rice, is a musical telling the story of Eva Perón (1919-1952), the beautiful and charismatic wife of Argentinian president Juan Perón.

Eva Perón was born in poverty in a small village but became a popular actress and later a politician with a reputation for helping the poor and downtrodden. She was mourned by millions on her death and went down into legend as one of the great public figures of latin America.

Evita started out not on stage but as a rock concept album. One of the songs, *Don't Cry for Me, Argentina* became a number one hit in 1976, and Lloyd Webber realised a stage musical could also be a big success.

He was correct: *Evita* opened at the Prince Edward Theatre on 21 June 1978 and closed on 18 February 1986, after 3,176 performances. Newcomer Elaine Paige played Eva with popular chart singer David Essex as Che, the narrator, and Joss Ackland as Perón.

Official portrait of Eva Perón, 'Evita'.

Solomons go solo

Independence for Pacific island chain

The Solomon Islands, in the Pacific Ocean to the north of of Australia, achieved independence from Great Britain on 7 July 1978.

The islands are probably best known for being the scene of some of the Second World War's bloodiest fighting, particularly at Guadalcanal, the first major allied offensive against Japan. The islands were also the temporary home of future US President John F Kennedy, who was shipwrecked there when serving with the US Navy.

In the post-war era it became increasingly expensive for Britain to directly govern the Solomons, and following the independence of neighbouring Papua New Guinea from Australia in 1975, it was decided to grant the islands independence within the Commonwealth, with Queen Elizabeth II as head of state, and Sir Peter Kenilorea as PM.

In 2012 the islands were visited by the Duke and Duchess of Cambridge to mark the sixtieth anniversary of the Queen's accession.

Clash of the tennis titans

Borg beats Connors at Wimbledon

Legendary tennis players Björn Borg and Jimmy Connors, who met 23 times in their careers, had the tennis battle of the year in July 1978 when they contested the Wimbledon mens' trophy.

Borg had already beaten Connors the previous year and did it again in '78, claiming his third straight Wimbledon title.

Undaunted, Connors defeated Borg two months later in a straight set final at the US Open. The pair would continue to clash on the courts until 1983.

Björn Borg with (inset) Jimmy Connors.

First of six million

The world's first 'test tube baby' is born

Over six million babies are estimated to have been born as a result of IVF (*in vitro* fertilisation), and it all started at Oldham General Hospital in the north of England on 25 July 1978 when Louise Joy Brown was born.

Louise's mother had been unable to conceive by conventional means and the couple decided to try a radical new treatment, where one of Mrs Brown's eggs was fertilized in a laboratory procedure using a petri dish (the term 'test tube' was a misnomer by journalists). It was then returned to the body to develop into a foetus in the normal manner. To huge media interest, Louise was delivered by planned caesarean section and was a normal healthy baby, weighing 5lb 12oz.

The IVF process was pioneered by British doctors Patrick Steptoe (1913-1988) and Robert Edwards (1925-2013). Edwards received the Nobel Prize for his work in 2010.

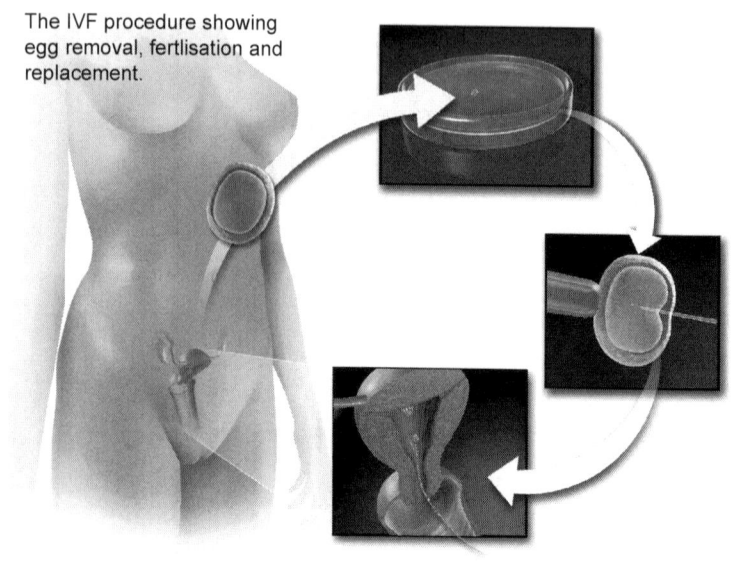

The IVF procedure showing egg removal, fertlisation and replacement.

Bruce Blaus

The *Double Eagle* has landed

First successful balloon crossing of the Atlantic

On 17 August 1978 the culmination of more than a century of effort took place when the first balloon successfully crossed the Atlantic, making an emergency landing in a barley field on the outskirts of Paris, France.

Aeronauts Ben Abruzzo, Maxie Anderson and Larry Newman had flown the *Double Eagle II* from Presque Isle, Maine, USA, taking 177 hours and six minutes to make the gruelling and dangerous crossing of the ocean.

The French authorities had expected them to land at Le Bourget, where previous pioneer Charles Lindbergh had ended the first solo powered flight in 1927. The crew of the *Double Eagle* realised that they were rapidly losing height, and it would be too risky to attempt to cross Paris where a sudden forced landing could have had serious consequences.

The flight was the fourteenth known attempt at the remarkable feat. Five aeronauts were killed or missing presumed dead in the previous crossings.

The *Double Eagle* crew were received in triumph at the US Embassy in Paris where they drew lots to sleep in the same bed as used by Lindbergh, and returned home in considerably greater comfort, on *Concorde.*

Model of the balloon at Presque Isle, Maine

Death of a gentleman

Actor Charles Boyer dies aged 78

One of the great actors of the 'old school', Frenchman Charles Boyer, died on 26 August 1978, aged 78.

Boyer discovered a talent to entertain while working as a hospital orderly during the First World War, putting on sketches to entertain the troops. He became a theatrical actor in the 1920s, also taking part in silent films, but his big break came with the arrival of the 'talkies' as he was able to exploit his excellent speaking and singing voice. Despite short stature, a paunch and a balding head, Boyer was cast as the romantic lead in many films, including *Algiers* and *All This and Heaven Too*. His career lasted much longer than most leading men, and he was still acting into the 1970s. Later films included *Barefoot in the Park* and *Around the World in Eighty Days*.

It is said that Boyer was also the inspiration for the romantically inclined French cartoon skunk, 'Pepe Le Pew'!

Boyer with co-star Elsa Martinelli in *The Rogues* (1964)

Markov murdered

Bulgarian dissident killed with poisoned umbrella

Markov was poisoned on Waterloo Bridge.

A shocking murder straight from the pages of a spy thriller took place in London on Georgi Ivanov Markov, (born 1929) was a dissident writer who had defected from Bulgaria due to his criticisms of that country's ruling regime.

Originally a popular novelist and playwright, Markov's work became more and more critical of the state authorities, and his novel *The Roof* was banned while it was still being printed. In 1969 Markov travelled to Italy and later London where he claimed asylum and started working for the BBC World Service.

On 7 September 1978 Markov walked across Waterloo Bridge in London and, while waiting at a bus stop, was stabbed with the point of an umbrella. Although suspicious at the time, the pain was not great and he ignored the incident. Later that day however he began to feel ill and was admitted to hospital, where he died four days later from Ricin poisoning, probably injected via the umbrella tip.

British authorities investigated but no killer has ever been found; in later years defectors claimed that the kill was carried out by the KGB. In 2005 the *Times* newspaper named the assassin as one, Francesco Gullino, known by the codename 'Piccadilly'. He was questioned by the British police but later released without charge.

Vicious ending

Former Sex Pistols frontman charged with murder

Sid Vicious making one of his final appearances with the Sex Pistols.

Punk band the Sex Pistols took the late 1970s by storm, with a series of controversial TV appearances and off-camera antics. The troubled band reached a low point early in 1978 when frontman Sid Vicious (real name John Ritchie) left the band to pursue a solo career with girlfriend and manager Nancy Spungeon.

On 12 October 1978 Vicious claimed to have woken from a drugged stupor to find Spungen dead on the bathroom floor of their room at the Hotel Chelsea in Manhattan. She had died from a stab wound made by a knife belonging to Vicious. He was arrested and charged with her murder, claiming the death was an accident.

Vicious was bailed and ten days later attempted to kill himself twice. On 9 December he was arrested again and for his own protection sent to prison. Released from jail on 1 February 1979, Vicious overdosed on heroin and was found dead by his mother the following day.

Hunt for the child killers

Britain shocked by paperboy murder

A murder which shocked the nation, and which has still never been satisfactorily solved, took place on 19 September 1978 when 12 year old schoolboy Carl Bridgewater was shot dead while on his paper round at Yew Tree Farm, near Stourbridge, West Midlands.

The police theorised that Carl accidentally disturbed a burglary, and was forced into the house where he was shot at close range with a shotgun.

Four men, dubbed the 'Bridgewater Four' were later arrested for the crime, Patrick Molloy, James Robinson, Michael Hickey and Vincent Hickey. All were convicted of murder except Molloy, who was charged with manslaughter as it was proved he was in another room during the murder.

However, in 1997, an appeal saw the convictions overturned and the three men released (Molloy died in prison in 1981), due to concerns about police handling of the evidence.

Several theories have been raised about the true killer of Carl, but no further convictions have been made.

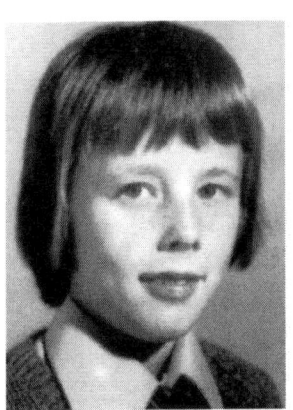

Twelve year old paperboy Carl Bridgewater was shot at close range at Yew Tree Farm in a case which has never been solved.

Christ in Liverpool
Britain's largest cathedral completed

Mention 'Liverpool cathedral' and most people think of the modernist Roman Catholic cathedral. The city however has two: the other is the Anglican Cathedral Church of Christ in Liverpool, which was consecrated on 25 October 1978 after 74 years in construction.

The cathedral was designed by Giles Gilbert Scott, who remarkably was only 22 and had no other buildings to his credit. He is perhaps best known for designing the iconic red British telephone box in the 1930s. He had a good sense of traditional medieval design, however, and produced a neo-gothic building fit for the modern age. Two world wars, with bomb damage in the second, hampered progress, and Scott died in 1960 so did not live to see the cathedral's completion. His son Richard carried on the work but eventually, a simpler design was used for the remaining parts.

The cathedral is the biggest in Britain as well as the country's largest religious building, and also boasts one of the largest bell towers in the world.

Death in the West Midlands

Five killed in shooting rampage

Five people were killed on 26 October 1978 when gunman Barry Williams went on the rampage. Williams (1944-2014) was a metal foundry worker and had been a member of a local gun club where he was nicknamed 'the Cowboy', eventually being asked to leave after concerns that he was stealing ammunition.

He had become involved in a number of disputes with neighbours, including one in which he made death threats. On the evening of 26 October he calmly walked around his West Bromwich neighbourhood shooting at random, killing five people and wounding several others. Williams was eventually tracked down and arrested by unarmed police after a high speed car chase.

Following his trial Williams was ordered to be detained at Broadmoor Hospital for the criminally insane, from which he was eventually released in 1994, considered no longer a threat.

In a disturbing twist, in 2013 Williams (renamed Harry Street) was again involved in harrassment of neighbours, who had no idea who he really was. Eventually police were called, and found a cache of guns and explosives in Street's house, following which Street was sent to a secure hospital indefinitely.

Now is the winter of our discontent
Industrial disputes spread across Britain

The winter of 1978/79 has gone down in history as one of the worst periods of industrial relations in British history, so much so that journalists dubbed it 'the winter of discontent', borrowing Shakespeare's quote alluding to the disastrous Wars of the Roses.

The winter saw widespread strikes by public sector trade unions demanding pay increases, which had been prevented by the pay caps of James Callaghan's Labour government which tried to keep pay rises under 5% in order to control rampant inflation.

Some of the more notorious strikes were those of gravediggers in Liverpool, meaning the dead went unburied for several weeks, and rubbish collectors in several cities, particularly London where Leicester Square was used as a makeshift dumping ground for huge amounts of uncollected rubbish. National Health Service workers also went on strike, meaning that many hospitals could only take emergency patients; a situation which worsened as the weather turned its coldest since 1963.

Many strikes dragged on into February 1979 when the Trade Union Council (TUC) instructed its members to go back to work.

The effect of the strikes on the Labour party's popularity was long-lived; the rival Conservative Party led by Margaret Thatcher won the 1979 election and was in power until 1997.

Prime Minister James Callaghan

End of an artistic era
Illustrator Norman Rockwell dies aged 84

Norman Rockwell, one of the giants of twentieth century illustration, died on 8 November 1978.

Rockwell was known for his inspiring and amusing illustrations for the *Saturday Evening Post*, which he created over five decades.

He is perhaps best known for his 'Four Freedoms' series (including 'Freedom From Want', above) which celebrated the American way of life. Rockwell was a prolific artist, producing over 4000 original works including portraits of Presidents Eisenhower, Kennedy, Johnson and Nixon.

He was very active in the Boy Scout movement and produced covers for their publication *Boys' Life* as well as Scouting calendars. Serious critics of the day often disliked Rockwell's work, describing it as overly sentimental, but he has gone down in history as an accomplished and popular artist.

Sadly many of his original canvases were destroyed in a fire in 1943, but they live on in numerous printed versions.

The Jonestown Massacre

918 dead in cult suicide

The Reverend Jim Jones was the sinister leader of the People's Temple cult.

One of the largest mass suicides in history took place on 18 November 1978 when 918 members of the People's Temple cult took poison at Jonestown in northwestern Guyana. Many of the cult members were US citizens and therefore this constituted the largest loss of American civilian life until the terrorist attacks of 11 September 2001.

The Peoples' Temple was set up in Indianapolis, Indiana, in 1955 by the sinister and charismatic clergyman James Warren Jones. After complaints about his conduct Jones moved his temple to a remote part of Guyana.

By the late 1970s media reports were circulating of human rights abuses in the temple. US Congressman Leo Ryan led a delegation to the commune and was shot dead while attempting to leave.

Knowing that the game was up, Jones encouraged his followers to drank Kool-Aid poisoned with cyanide. Jones himself was later found dead after apparently shooting himself.

'Killer Clown' captured

Serial killer John Wayne Gacy arrested

Known as the 'killer clown' because he worked as a childrens' entertainer, serial murderer John Wayne Gacy was finally captured on 22 December 1978.

Gacy (1942-1994) tortured and killed at least 33 teenage boys and young men between 1972 and 1978 at his house at Norwood Park, Illinois. The victims were buried under his house or thrown into the nearby Des Plaines River.

In March 1978, one of Gacy's victims, Jeffrey Rignall, managed to escape from Gacy's house but could not remember the location as Gacy had drugged him. He did, however, remember Gacy's car and police were able to track down the owner. The authorities were suspicious of Gacy but lacked evidence, and so he was put under observation. Eventually they received reports from a suspicious workman that Gacy had asked him to spread lime in his basement, and police decided to search the property.

On entering the basement of his house, horrified detectives realised that dozens of bodies had been buried there. Gacy brought to trial on 6 February 1980. Doctors ruled that he was sane and he was sentenced to death; following years of appeals this sentence was carried out on 9 May 1994. Gacy showed no remorse.

Twisted killer John Wayne Gacy and his chilling alter-ego, 'Pogo the Clown'.

YMCA

Smash hit for the Village People

The Village People's 1978 song *YMCA* was their greatest hit.

YMCA by the Village People was one of the biggest hits of 1978/79. It is one of fewer than 40 singles to have sold over ten million physical copies worldwide, and became the group's biggest hit.

The song remains popular, particularly at sporting events, probably in part due to its easy to remember dance movements which spell out the letters of the title. The song refers to the international organisation the Young Mens' Christian Association, which created a certain amount of controversy for the group. Known to have a large gay following, it was alleged that the Village People were referring to the YMCA as a place for homosexual pick-ups.

The YMCA initially threatened to sue the band for using its name but later expressed pride in the song. The Village People's lyricist, Victor Willis, described the song as a celebration of the YMCA as a popular and fun leisure destination for urban youth.

BIRTHDAY NOTEBOOKS

FROM
MONTPELIER PUBLISHING

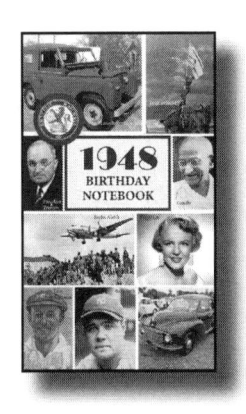

Handy 60-page ruled notebooks with a significant event of the year on each page.

A great alternative to a birthday card.
Available from Amazon.

Printed in Great Britain
by Amazon